INVINCIBLE

FATHERS AND MOTHERS OF BLACK AMERICA

WADE HUDSON ART BY E. B. LEWIS

CALKINS CREEK

AN IMPRINT OF ASTRA BOOKS FOR YOUNG READERS

New York

To all those brave Black pioneers who built what we now know as Black America: we will never forget!

From Africa they were captured.

Chained and crammed into the hulls of ships, they were human cargo destined to be sold like goods that men purchase with care.

Mandinka. Fon. Bakongo. Chamba. Abron. Fulani.
Akan. Wolof. Igbo. Yoruba. Mbundu.

They spoke different languages, yet the spirit of Africa beat in all their hearts.

Enslaved to work the fields of the "New World," to raise the white masters' children,

to cook their meals, to build their houses
and cities, they helped create a nation.

Restrictive laws sought to determine their fate.
Brutal treatment was their constant companion.

Yet they fought back with whatever means they could muster.

See them mounting rebellions.
See them running away.
See them refusing to work.
See them in the courtroom suing for freedom.
See them handing out pamphlets that declare
their right to be free.

"Let freedom ring!" became the refrain in the colonies.

It rang when the Declaration of Independence was signed in 1776.

It continued to ring when the Revolutionary War was won in 1783 and a Constitution was soon established.

But freedom didn't ring for all.

It didn't ring for the enslaved or for those who had bought or won their freedom or who had escaped from slavery.

It didn't ring for women, Indigenous people, or the poor.

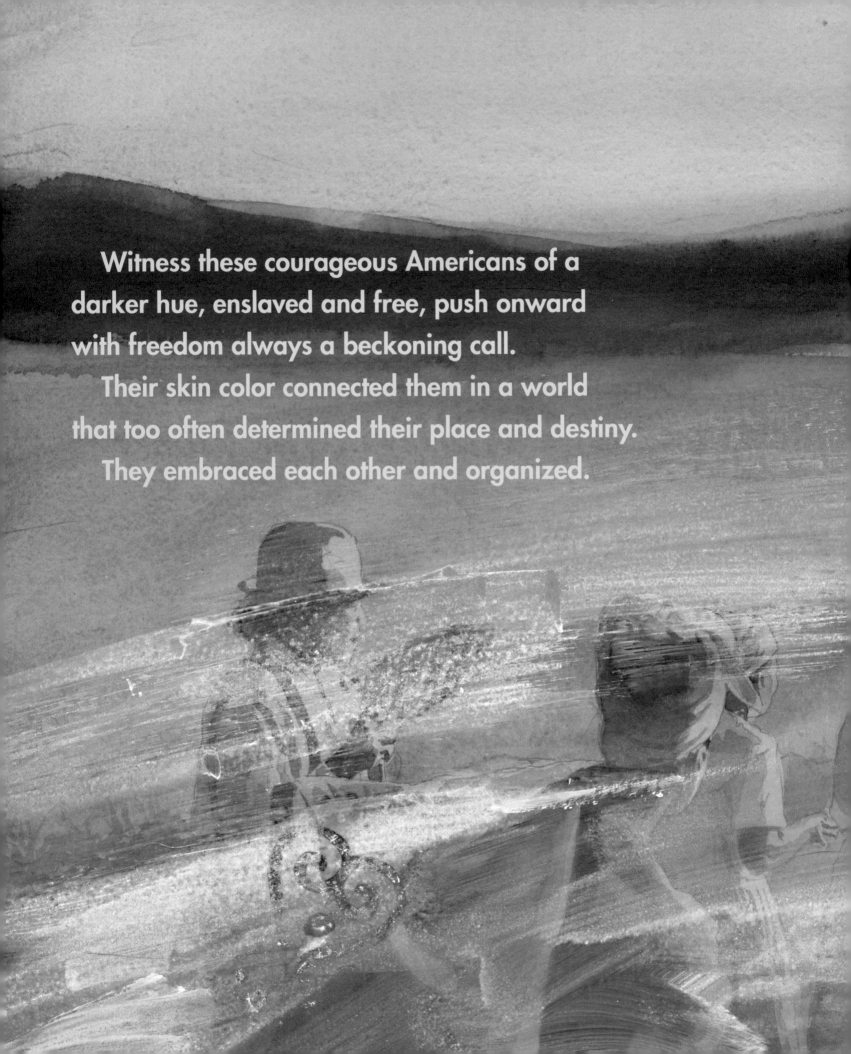

Witness these courageous Americans of a darker hue, enslaved and free, push onward with freedom always a beckoning call.

Their skin color connected them in a world that too often determined their place and destiny.

They embraced each other and organized.

Year by year, organization by organization, contribution by contribution, they built and grew, pushed and pulled, overcame and withstood.

Before long, they had created Black America—a Black consciousness and Black institutions, where they could live, do, create, produce, inspire, and soar.

Black America was a place for them to be!

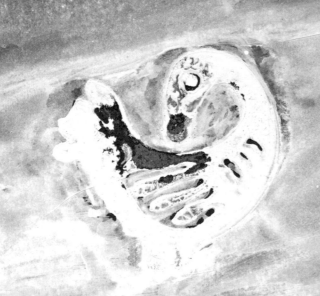

So they continued to build . . .

1738: The first free African community is established at Fort Mose in Florida.

1760s: Jupiter Hammon and Phillis Wheatley put pen to paper writing poems.

1770s: Among the first Black churches formally organized in the United States were the First African Baptist Church in Savannah, Georgia; the Silver Bluff Baptist Church in Silver Bluff, South Carolina; and the First Baptist Church in Petersburg, Virginia. African Americans, however, held informal church services decades earlier.

1784: Prince Hall founds Freemason African Lodge Number 459 in Boston. Groups in Philadelphia, New York City, and New Haven, Connecticut, follow, making the Masons the first Black fraternal national organization.

1787: The New York African Free School opens its doors.

1787: In Philadelphia, Richard Allen and Absalom Jones form the Free African Society to help meet the educational, social, and spiritual needs of their community.

1791: Astronomer Benjamin Banneker helps survey the original borders of Washington, DC.

1793: The Benevolent Female Society of St. Thomas is organized to oversee programs to help the poor and needy, a responsibility that had been previously handled by the Free African Society.

1794: Richard Allen establishes the Mother Bethel African Methodist Episcopal (AME) Church in Philadelphia. His wife, Sarah, creates the Daughters of the Conference to assist the church's ministers in 1827.

1798: James Forten purchases a loft and starts his own sail-making business. He becomes a leading businessman in Philadelphia. Paul Cuffe has already built a successful shipping business in Massachusetts.

1800s: Most of the free African Americans in Boston live in an area now called the North Slope of Beacon Hill. In this thriving community, the residents are active in the Underground Railroad and fight the racism and discrimination they face daily.

1810: Israel Hill, a Black community in Farmville, Virginia, is organized. The community is started by approximately ninety men and women who received freedom and 350 acres from the will of Richard Randolph, a cousin of Thomas Jefferson. These free African Americans work as farmers, craftspeople, river boatmen, sell real estate, and found the town's first Baptist church in 1836.

1819: Jarena Lee delivers a sermon at Mother Bethel AME Church, becoming the first African American woman to preach the Gospel.

1821: The African Grove Theatre, founded and operated by William Alexander Brown, opens in New York City. The esteemed Black Shakespearian actor Ira Aldridge makes his stage debut there.

1825: Seneca Village, one of the first Black communities in New York City, is founded. At its peak, the community has approximately 225 residents, three churches, two schools, and three cemeteries. The settlement is later also inhabited by Irish and German immigrants and exists until 1857, when it is destroyed to make way for the construction of Central Park.

1827: Samuel E. Cornish and John B. Russwurm publish the first Black newspaper, *Freedom's Journal.*

1830: The first national African American convention to address slavery, racism, and education is held in Philadelphia at the Mother Bethel AME Church.

1831: Sarah Mapps Douglass, educator, abolitionist, and artist, helps found the Female Literary Association for African American women to discuss social and political issues of the day.

For themselves, for their children, for those to come, they continued to build and grow. These fathers and mothers of Black America pressed on to create THEIR own places to BE!

So, when you see the nobility of a Black organization, think of these eminent men and women.

When you enjoy the blues, soul, rap, and spirituals, think of them.

When you hear a dynamic orator in the Black tradition, think of them!

When you read inspiring words penned by Black writers, think of them.

When you purchase items from Black-owned businesses, think of them.

When you hear the rallying cry, "Black Lives Matter," think of them, too.

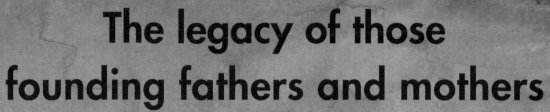

The legacy of those founding fathers and mothers

of Black America
still inspires today!

AUTHOR'S NOTE

In school, I learned about the Founding Fathers who fought for American freedom. These were the men who wrote the Declaration of Independence, drafted a constitution, established the foundation for the new nation, and, on September 9, 1776, named that new nation the United States of America. To a young boy fascinated by history, these men, George Washington, Thomas Jefferson, Benjamin Franklin, Alexander Hamilton, and James Madison, were larger than life. Without them, and others like them, declared the books that I read, there would be no United States of America.

These men were not just featured in school textbooks and biographies I found in our small school library. Movies and television dramas presented their stories and showcased important events in the founding of the country. Like many youngsters, I watched these productions intently. Women, Black Americans and people of color were rarely included as important players in these historical stories. I was not at that time aware of how distorted and sanitized these renderings were.

I knew very little about the extent of the enslavement of African people and the role it played in weaving the political, economic, and social fabric of the country. People from Africa were not only seen as inferior by most white people, but as subhuman, a belief they felt justified and sanctioned their brutal treatment and enslavement of Black people.

In 1857, Roger B. Taney, Chief Justice of the United States Supreme Court, rubber-stamped this belief from the bench of the highest court in the land. In the *Dred Scott v. Sandford* decision, he wrote that at the time of the writing of the US Constitution:

> *[Black people] had for more than a century before been regarded as beings of an inferior order, and altogether unfit to associate with the white race, either in social or political relations; and so far inferior, that they had no rights which the white man was bound to respect; and that the negro might justly and lawfully be reduced to slavery for his benefit. He was bought and sold, treated as an ordinary article of merchandise and traffic, whenever a profit could be made by it.*

Chief Justice Taney articulated and affirmed the centuries-old belief on which this nation was built. It gave support and sanction to the enslavement of Black people and justified the harsh, dehumanizing treatment meted out to them even after slavery ended in 1865.

How did Black people respond to this systemic mistreatment? How did they respond to their enslavement? What about those who were able to free themselves from slavery? How did they deal with the discrimination and violence they faced constantly, including from slave catchers who sought to enslave them?

Just as the Founding Fathers of America fought for independence and established a new nation, Black Americans set their sights on freedom, too. And because they were forbidden from participating in the life of white America, they formed their own communities, institutions, businesses, organizations, churches, schools, newspapers, and theaters and wrote and told their own stories. Their treatment was determined by skin color, and for them, it ordered their struggle and resistance. They perceived their shared African heritage and forged an identity based upon it. Names of institutions and organizations often included reference to that African heritage: African Lodge No. 459, African Meeting House, African Grove Theatre, African Methodist Episcopal Church. And they fought relentlessly to end slavery.

Despite all the obstacles, Black America grew even as America itself grew. And Black Americans not only contributed to their own growth but to that of America as well.

After slavery ended in 1865, Black Americans continued to build on what the Founding Fathers and Mothers of Black America had established. Nearly four million Black Americans newly freed from slavery established communities in cities across the United States. Some founded all-Black towns in the Midwest. Jim Crow (laws and customs that were racist and discriminatory and often enforced with violence) hampered their efforts

and made life difficult, but it couldn't stop what had begun many decades earlier.

I didn't know the historical significance of Black America when I was growing up. Of course, I knew there was a Black community, I lived in one. I knew there was a Black America. I saw it on the pages of Black magazines and newspapers and in the lives of Black people I knew. But I didn't know the history or people who established it.

So I am honored to share a few of the Founding Fathers and Mothers of Black America in this picture book. Just as there would be no United States of America without the Founding Fathers, there would be no Black America without these Founding Fathers and Mothers.

Very few artists can capture the humanity, character, resilience, and determination of Black people and the Black experience in America like E. B. Lewis. We have known each other for several decades, and I have always admired his extraordinary work. What an honor to partner with him to bring this important story to readers!

THE JOURNEY TO COMMUNITY

African Americans in Colonial America

Many cite 1619 as the year the first Africans were brought to Colonial America, where they became enslaved people or indentured servants in Virginia. Prior to 1619, however, Africans accompanied the Spanish to Florida and parts of the Southwest. Some were slaves, others were free.

Juan Garrido was the first documented African to arrive in the new land. He was a member of the crew of Juan Ponce de León, who came to Florida in 1513 in search of the Fountain of Youth. Later Estevanico, a man enslaved by the Spanish, became the first African to explore the southwestern part of the country during a trip that began in 1528 and lasted several years.

The Middle Passage

The Middle Passage is a term that describes the transporting of enslaved Africans from the African continent on slave ships across the Atlantic Ocean to the Americas.

During the 15th, 16th, and 17th centuries, Europeans built forts along the West Coast of Africa, where they traded rum, cloth, guns, and other goods for captured Africans. Forced to walk hundreds of miles in shackles, these Africans were imprisoned in dungeons at the forts where they remained in horrible conditions until slave ships arrived to take them to South, Central, and North America where they were sold into chattel slavery.

It is estimated that more than twenty million Africans were captured and taken from their homelands. Millions perished, and countless communities were devastated.

Establishing Slavery with Slave Codes

After 1619, more and more Africans were brought to Colonial America to work the growing tobacco, rice, and indigo plantations in the Southern colonies. In 1705, the Virginia General Assembly passed a law that legalized the enslavement of Africans in America. It said in part:

> *All servants imported and brought into the Country . . . who were not Christians in their native Country . . . shall be accounted and be slaves. All Negro, mulatto and Indian slaves within this dominion . . . shall be held to be real estate. If any slave resists his master . . . correcting such slave, and shall happen to be killed in such correction . . . the master shall be free of all punishment . . . as if such accident never happened.*

Thousands of slave laws or codes were enacted across the colonies, firmly establishing the institution of slavery in America.

Life Under Slavery

Life for most enslaved men and women was brutal and harsh. Families were frequently separated when members were sold to other plantation owners, often in states far away. Slave owners prescribed whipping for minor offenses and they branded, mutilated, and even murdered enslaved African Americans for what they considered more serious offenses. Militias of free white men called slave patrols were used to enforce the strict slave codes that regulated every aspect of the lives of enslaved persons.

Large plantations had field hands who worked the expansive cotton, rice, and tobacco fields, as well as house servants, who did the cooking, cleaning, and taking care of the plantation owner's family. Enslaved Black persons were also forced to work as carpenters, millwrights, stone cutters, glazers, horsemen, factory workers, and seamstresses. The enslaved population in the United States grew from around 700,000 in 1790 to more than 3,900,000 in 1860, around the time the Civil War began.

Fighting Back

Enslaved Black people did not accept their fate without protest. They resisted slavery in a variety of active and passive ways. Breaking tools, feigning illness, staging slowdowns, and committing acts of arson and sabotage were common forms of resistance. Many ran away to freedom to Canada or states in the North that had banned slavery. Some who escaped formed communities in remote areas of the South. They organized numerous rebellions. A few even purchased their freedom when more lenient slave masters permitted them to secure paid jobs after they had finished their work on the plantation.

Free African Americans

Some African Americans acquired free status as early as the late 1600s. Freedom was gained in different ways. Sometimes, male slave owners freed children they fathered with enslaved Black women. Some enslaved persons secured their freedom as a reward for fighting in wars and conflicts such as the Revolutionary War. A few used the courts to escape from slavery. Most who achieved freedom, however, did so by running away.

The first national census taken in the country in 1790 revealed nearly 60,000 African Americans who were free. Most lived in the North, especially in Philadelphia, New York City, and Boston. Those in the South lived in cities such as Charleston, South Carolina; New Orleans, Louisiana; and Atlanta, Georgia. By the time the Civil War started in 1861, there were nearly 500,000 free African Americans living in the United States.

Freedom Papers

Legally free African Americans were required to register with county courts and secure Certificates of Freedom, also known as freedom papers. Many who had run away could not get a freedom paper. So, they had to remain underground, always fearful of being caught and enslaved again.

African American Communities

Most free African Americans were forced to live in their own communities, separate from white communities. They faced discrimination in almost all areas of their lives. Most were not permitted to vote. They had to sit in segregated cars on trains or stand if there were no separate cars for them. Their legal rights were often not respected by the courts. On the streets, they were attacked by white people. But these communities gave rise to the establishment of Black institutions, Black culture, Black creativity, and Black identity and provided the infrastructure for a Black America. Those who lived in these communities were the vanguard in the fight to end slavery and racial injustice.

African American Organizations

Richard Allen and Absalom Jones established one of the first mutual aid organizations in Philadelphia in 1787. The Free African Society provided social and economic guidance and medical care, and helped newly arrived Black people become accustomed to their new life. It acquired land for a graveyard, performed and recorded marriages, and documented births for its community.

Other mutual aid organizations included the Brown Fellowship Society, established on November 1, 1790 in Charleston, South Carolina, and Economy Hall, established in 1836 in New Orleans. These organizations and hundreds of others like them helped to give structure to Black communities.

The African American Church

Churches have been the most enduring and transformative institutions in Black American life. One of the earliest was the First African Baptist Church of Savannah, Georgia, founded by George Liele in 1777. Mother Bethel African Methodist Episcopal Church was founded by Richard Allen in 1794. By 1820, there were dozens of Black churches in the North and South representing four denominations, including the African Methodist Episcopal Church, the first Black one organized in the country.

Not only did Black churches serve the spiritual needs of their followers, they also offered a place where cultural and artistic activities could take place, established schools, and were at the forefront of the struggle for freedom and an end to slavery. Black preachers were often the unquestioned leaders of their communities. The Black church was the lifeblood of a burgeoning Black America in the late 1700s and early 1800s.

African American Schools

Although education was prohibited by many state and local laws, African Americans, enslaved or free, recognized its importance. Those who were enslaved often risked their lives to learn how to read and write. Primus Hall, the son of Prince Hall, founder of Black

Freemasonry, established a school in his home in 1798. In 1787, a little over a decade before Primus Hall started his school, the New York Manumission (freedom from slavery) Society founded the one-room New York African Free School with thirty African American children whose parents were enslaved or had escaped bondage. Many African American churches, such as Mother Bethel Church in Philadelphia and the First African Baptist Church in Boston, also operated schools.

African American Businesses

Despite racial discrimination, some free African Americans were able to establish professional careers and businesses, mostly in their own communities.

Most free African American men, however, were laborers, while many free African American women worked as domestic servants in the homes of white families. But despite racial discrimination and resentment, some African Americans also were able to carve out careers as hairdressers, barbers, wigmakers, tailors, seamstresses, milliners, food caterers, and dressmakers. A few established successful businesses. James Forten invented a sail-making device that enabled him to create a very profitable enterprise that was worth an estimated $100,000, which is equivalent to more than $2 million today. Paul Cuffe and his brother-in-law started a successful shipping business in Westport, Massachusetts. Cuffe was also a prosperous merchant,

farmer, and the largest employer of African Americans. He was one of the wealthiest African Americans of his time. Black entrepreneurs William Whipper and Stephen Smith created one of Pennsylvania's most successful lumberyards. In 1825, the formerly enslaved Thomas Dowling opened the Oyster House, which would become one of the most successful restaurants in New York City. These men, and others like them, used their wealth to help other African Americans. They were leaders in the abolitionist movement that sought to end slavery and helped to build an emerging Black America.

SOURCES

Bennett Jr., Lerone. *Before the Mayflower: A History of Black America.* New York: Penguin Books, 1993.

———. *Pioneers in Protest.* Chicago: Johnson Publishing Company Inc., 1968.

———. *The Shaping of Black America.* Chicago: Johnson Publishing Company Inc., 1975.

Franklin, John Hope and Alfred A. Moss Jr. *From Slavery to Freedom: A History of African Americans.* New York: Alfred A. Knopf, 2000.

Harding, Vincent. *There Is A River: The Struggle for Black Freedom in America.* New York: Mariner Books, 1993.

Mullane, Deirdre. *Crossing the Danger Water: Three Hundred Years of African-American Writing.* New York: Anchor Books, 1993.

Painter, Nell Irvin. *Creating Black Americans: African-American History and Its Meanings, 1619 to the Present.* New York: Oxford University Press, 2006.

Quarles, Benjamin. *The Negro in the Making of America,* 3rd ed. New York: Touchstone Book, 1996.

ACKNOWLEDGMENTS

I wish to thank E. B. Lewis, not only for his dynamic and powerful illustrations that give life to this book, but also for the conversations that inspired writing it. We share the common goal of portraying Black people realistically, as fully human, with strengths and weaknesses, and as the heroes and heroines that many of them are.

I thank Carolyn Yoder, my editor, for her direction and insight in helping to make this important book that spotlights a crucial part of Black history a reality.

I also thank my wife and partner, Cheryl Willis Hudson, for her support and feedback that help to make any endeavor I undertake so much better.

Lastly, I thank the ancestors, those who helped make it possible for me to do what I love. Ashe!

ARTIST'S NOTE

I have incorporated the Sankofa bird into my artwork. It is a powerful symbol of the Akan people of Ghana and can be found throughout the world, including the early days of Black America, in many contexts.

The Sankofa bird is shown with her head looking back to the past while holding a precious egg in her beak. Her feet point straight ahead toward the future. The Akan see the past as a guide to the future. A strong future means learning from the past. *San* means "return"; *ko* means "go"; and *fa* means "look and take." The bird reminds us to return to the past and bring what is good to the present, and then through knowledge and truth make progress.

The Sankofa bird also symbolizes respect and unity.

For me, the Sankofa reminds us that history should not be segregated but shared. Since 1619, the horrific details of the lives of the enslaved have been stuffed into the closet of American history. Because of this, WE the descendants of both the "enslaved" as well as the "enslaver" have been denied the truth of what our families had to endure. If we as a nation do not understand how we arrived in the present, the nation will never be healthy.

The paintings in this book depict a graphic truth with the colors of urgency. They should be shown as independent works of art and hopefully will inspire honest conversations about our shared history.

Dedicated to the Black pioneers and trailblazers
who founded Black America, forged a national Black
identity, and helped to build the United States
of America — *WH*

To the strength and resilience of those more than
6,000,000 enslaved ancestors who helped build
this country — *EBL*

For information about permissions to reproduce
selections from this book, please contact
permissions@astrapublishinghouse.com.

Calkins Creek
An imprint of Astra Books for Young Readers,
a division of Astra Publishing House
astrapublishinghouse.com
Printed in China

ISBN: 978-1-63592-509-8 (hc)
ISBN: 978-1-63592-544-9 (eBook)
Library of Congress Control Number: 2022948002

First edition
10 9 8 7 6 5 4 3 2 1

Designed by Barbara Grzeslo
The type is set in Futura STD heavy.
The art is done in watercolor and gouache on paper.